From Hurt... To Healed

Unmasking the Pain to Walk in Freedom

Dr. Carrie Motley

ROYSTON
Publishing

BK Royston Publishing
P. O. Box 4321
Jeffersonville, IN 47131
502-802-5385
http://www.bkroystonpublishing.com
bkroystonpublishing@gmail.com

© Copyright – 2021

All Rights Reserved. No part of this book may be reproduced, stored in a retrieval system, or transmitted by any means without the written permission of the author.

Cover Design: Elite Covers
Cover Photo: Norman Turner Photography

ISBN-13: 978-1-951941-92-5

King James Version (KJV) Public Domain

New International Version (NIV) Holy Bible, New International Version®, NIV® Copyright ©1973, 1978, 1984, 2011 by Biblica, Inc.® Used by permission. All rights reserved worldwide. NIV Reverse Interlinear Bible: English to Hebrew and English to Greek. Copyright © 2019 by Zondervan.

New International Reader's Version (NIRV) Copyright © 1995, 1996, 1998, 2014 by Biblica, Inc.®. Used by permission. All rights reserved worldwide.

Printed in the United States of America

Dedication

I Dedicate This Book To
My Loving Husband and Children:
Dennis, Alaina, and Perrion Motley

My Dear Mother:
Mother Elaine Reed

My brothers and sisters:
Pastor David A. Reed (Iris), Vanessa Beatty (Rick), Marsha Sokolow (John), Gayle Thomas (Danny), Joe Reed (Laurie), Rodriquez Reed (Jackie), Mondell Reed (Ebony), and Tamela McClinton (Pastor James McClinton)

My Godmother:
Arie Williams

My nieces and nephews

My special cousin/sister:
Martha Fuller

Reed's Temple Church Hospitality Sisters

In Loving Memory Of

My Father:

Overseer Joe B. Reed Sr.

My Sister:

Vera Ellen Reed (Pay Pay)

Acknowledgments

I thank my Lord and Savior Jesus Christ for inspiring me to write this book.

To my loving husband and biggest supporter Dennis Motley, who lovingly encouraged me throughout this process.

To my children, Alaina and Perrion Motley, for patiently lending their ear, and for all of their support.

To my dear mother, my prayer partner, Mother Elaine Reed who prayed me through.

To my pastor and brother Admin. Asst. David A. Reed who allowed me the use of Reed's Temple Church for photos.

Special Thanks

To my sisters—Gayle Thomas, Tamela McClinton (Mgr) and Goddaughter Stacy Young (Mgr)—for being a listening ear, and for their encouragement.

To my brother—Rodriquez Reed who was a listening ear for this project but didn't realize it.

To my best friend—Vernita Cousin who recognized what God had given me was a book.

BK Royston Publishing LLC—who was very instrumental in my completion of this book.

Norman Turner Photography—Photographer

Table of Contents

Dedication	iii
In Loving Memory	v
Acknowledgements	vii
Special Thanks	viii
Foreword	xi
Prologue	xv
Introduction	xvii
Chapter 1 From Teased to Pleased	1
Chapter 2 A Battle with Fear	15
Chapter 3 Dressed Up and Messed Up	21
Chapter 4 Hurt but Not Harmed	31
Chapter 5 Forgiveness Is Essential to Be Healed	45

Chapter 6 The Bruises of Life	53
Chapter 7 Just Because It Hurts Doesn't Mean It has to Dwell: "Give it to Jesus"	67
Conclusion	81
Healing Scriptures	87
A Call to Salvation	89

Foreword

I have had the privilege of knowing and working with Dr. Carrie Motley for several years. Truly, God's providence was at work when he allowed our paths to cross. She has been a trusted confidante, spiritual role model, and loving Godmother through some of the most challenging experiences of my adulthood. I am endlessly grateful for her presence in my life.

It has been my pleasure to witness the manifestation of God's spirit at work through her passion for ministry. She is a committed servant of God, with a heart for guiding believers toward spiritual maturity. It is not often that a person has the patience and grace needed to support those in the early stages of their walk with Christ, but Dr. Motley has been blessed with the gifts necessary to be a listening ear, sage advisor, and prayer partner to many Christians. Her love for others draws her to those in need, and it is that love that birthed this book into reality.

It is not easy, dear reader, to share the depth of personal struggle and calamity, but the book you hold in your hands is a transparent account of trials, tests, and triumphs. Dr. Motley relates her experiences with candor and sincerity so that others will know the power God has to see our needs and deliver us.

It is no accident that you picked up this book. Open your heart and mind to the possibility that this could be your turning point. Be honest with yourself, as Dr. Motley has been with us, and allow this message of healing to permeate your soul, shining the light of truth on darkened places.

Your journey to healing starts now.

Stacy Young

Prologue

Have you ever been hurt? I mean, really hurt—the kind of hurt that makes you feel all alone, hopeless, and like giving up—the kind of pain that keeps you up at night wondering "why me?" At different times in our lives, we may have experienced intense hurts, perhaps coming from different directions—the death of a loved one, the betrayal of a friend, failed or broken relationships, false accusations, and even self-inflicted wounds. We may wonder at times why life must be so painful and unfair. Given our own way, we may wish to escape the hurts of this world by abandoning our responsibilities or fleeing our difficult circumstances.

God, however, has a purpose for allowing hurt in our lives, and our healing and freedom is in our willingness to let go and give it to Jesus.

Introduction

Unmasking the Pain to Walk in Freedom

As I am writing this book, we are in the midst of a global pandemic. The Corona Virus also known as COVID-19, has hit the world and it has affected us greatly. Restaurants, malls, schools, and even churches have closed their doors due to this virus in hopes of containing the spread of it. This has definitely been a year of loss—loss of lives, loss of businesses, loss of fellowship—and so many seemingly have lost their faith. We are in a place in our lives where we have never been before. We have to maintain social distance; therefore, many are working from home. We even must wear masks in public. Some are struggling with wearing masks because it is uncomfortable. It's not always easy to breathe through them. The truth of the matter is some people have been wearing an uncomfortable invisible mask for years.

Why do people wear masks? Why do they try to hide their true selves? Why do they try to hide their hurt and their pain? For some, it's about self-image. Nothing is supposed to break them, yet they are broken on the inside. "A mask is something used to cover, in order to conceal, protect or disguise something or someone." (The free dictionary by Farlax) People don't always know who you are behind your mask. It's hard sometimes to even recognize you. You could be smiling, happy, sad, frowning, or even depressed behind the mask, and no one will ever know. Always remember that we see masks, but God sees hearts.

"Many times, in life, people mask themselves so others will see only what they want them to see, ultimately preventing them from seeing their bad side, their weaknesses, and their insecurities. Others wear a mask to forget. Many people think that if they put on a mask they won't have to deal with a painful past or even a current situation. The problem is that the thoughts will continue to chase you in one way or another and we will not forget." (Breaking the chains Biblical Recovery Ministry Warrior's Encampment). At some point in life, you have to take off the mask and deal with the pain. Acknowledge that you're hurting, and that the pain is still there from years of being either verbally or physically abused, falsely accused, or betrayed by a friend. What happened to you fifteen years ago, what they said to you ten months ago, what you experienced a few weeks ago—that hurt, and that pain is still there, and it is bleeding out through your behaviors. Your hurt will expose you. Get rid of the offense.

When you go to the doctor's office, they ask you a series of questions, so they are better able to treat your illness, injury, or your condition. If you come in with a pain they may ask, "where is the pain?" If the pain is in your back, you're not going to have them check your foot—or anywhere else on your body, for that matter. You are going to tell the doctor exactly where your pain is. The same way you share with your doctor about your pain, your aches, your symptoms, and how long you've experienced them is the same way you need to share your hurt and pain with God.

Tell God who hurt you, how long you have been hurting, and how it made you feel. God already knows all about you. He's omniscient. (He's all knowing.) However, he wants you to come to him and tell him about your hurt and your pain. You do not have to put on a façade with God. Why? Because he already knows, and he is the only one that can help you; he has the power and the wherewithal to change your situation and to change you. God can heal you if you can get to the point of believing. God loves you, and he is concerned about those things that concern you. There is no problem too big for him to solve for he is greater than anything that you can ever experience. Take off the mask, so you can walk in freedom and allow the Lord to heal you where you hurt.

From Teased to Pleased

Have you ever been teased or made fun of because you are unusual or different? It's not only a bad feeling for a child, but adults also struggle with this same discomfort. Today, we call it being bullied, but for the sake of this chapter, I am going to stick with calling it being teased. According to Merriam-Webster Dictionary, tease means "to make fun of, to disturb or annoy by persistent irritating or provoking especially in a petty or mischievous way." There is a saying that goes "Sticks and stones may break my bones, but words will never hurt me." I strongly disagree with this statement. Although words cannot cause physical harm, they can, however, damage you both emotionally and internally. They can damage your self-esteem, can hinder you from reaching your goals, and can cause you to give up. The tongue is so powerful that there are words spoken by those dead and gone that still hurt the living to this day. The Bible says in Proverbs 18:21 (KJV) "Death and life are in the power of the tongue: and they that love it shall eat the fruit thereof." Being hurt does not always instantly go away: it penetrates the heart of the wounded. We can use our words to build others up, or we can use our words to tear others down.

"You have the Sanctified Touch."

Growing up as a PK (Pastor's Kid) wasn't always a great experience for me. In grammar school, everyone just about knew that my father was a pastor. Our family went to church every Sunday, Tuesday, and Friday, in addition to revivals, rehearsals, Wednesday Prayer, teas and picnics, etc.

We grew up in an extremely strict home, and there were a lot of things that my siblings and I were not allowed to do. (We later found out that their strictness saved us—but that's another story). We couldn't go to the show, go bowling, and rarely could go visit family members' homes. My sisters and I weren't allowed to wear pants. We mostly wore the long prairie skirts, and because of me not being able to wear pants and being different, I was teased by the children at school.

This teasing went on from first to sixth grade. Oh, how well I remember. They would call me "the Sanctified Girl." "Here comes Miss Sanctified." Children can be so cruel. They got so good at it until they started playing a game. They would touch me and then touch someone else, cross their fingers and tell that person that they had the Sanctified Touch. For those reasons, a lot of my classmates didn't want to be around me, fearing that they too would be teased. I got tired of them teasing me. Sometimes because I was sensitive I would even cry.

When winter came and it got cold outside, my mom would allow me to put on a pair of my brother's pants under my skirt and she told me to take them off as soon as I got to school and put them back on at the end of the school day. However, with the long prairie skirts that I wore, no one would ever notice. One day I decided that maybe my classmates wouldn't tease me if I wore pants. So, I went to the bathroom this time and I took off the skirt and left the pants on. When I came out, they teased me even more. They said, "Look at the Sanctified Girl trying to wear pants. "You better go take those pants off because if your father come up here, you're going to be in trouble." They were right. I had the kind of parents who would just show up at the school at any given time unannounced. So, with a hurt heart, I went back in the bathroom changed back into my skirt.

I will never forget one guy, whom I will call "Classmate." He got in my face one day and said, "Ah ha, you're sanctified." I put my hands in his face and said, "You leave me alone." He looked at me and laughed so hard. He said, "Get your religious fingers out of my face." That day when I got home and rang the doorbell, my father answered the door. He noticed that I was down in spirits and he asked me what was bothering me. I explained to him that I was getting teased every day from the children at school and I was tired of it. He asked what they were saying. I shared with him that they would touch me and then touch someone else, cross their fingers, and say, "you got the sanctified touch." My father responded "Girl, you do have the sanctified touch. 'But as for me and my house we will serve the Lord'" (Joshua 24:15, KJV). It seemed that the harsh reality for me meant that I was going to have to deal with being teased.

My mother didn't make it any better, she is a prayer warrior. She would wait right until one of our favorite TV shows would come on, then say, "Turn off the TV It's time for all things," and we knew it was time to pray. Mom would not get off her knees until she felt the presence of God and of course, when she was done our TV shows would be over. Some of my classmates would tease and say, "We heard y'all praying last night."

When I got in the sixth grade, I knew that there was no out for me. One day I thought to myself, "I have to act saved at home, I have to act saved at church, and no matter what I do at school, in my classmates' eyes, I'm still sanctified." So, I decided to get saved for real.

No More Acting

On Friday nights, we would have tarrying service where we would go to the altar and call on Jesus. Well, August 21, 1982, I will never forget because I had a life-changing experience. We were about to tarry and right before, my father had different people testify about how they received the Holy Ghost. As they began to testify, it seemed their very words were captivating my soul. When the tarrying service began, my father told us to call on Jesus. After calling Jesus a couple of times, I could no longer speak for myself. The Holy Ghost began to speak through me (I spoke in tongues as the spirit of the Lord gave utterance). Oh, my God, I will never forget that day. I could hear my father excitedly saying, "Oh, she got the Holy Ghost."

I couldn't wait to go back to school to tell my classmates and teachers that I had received the Holy Ghost. I am not sure if they understood what that meant. However, I am sure that they knew that there was something different about me because I kept reminding them that I had the sanctified touch; they stopped reminding me. God used the teasing of my classmates to draw me to him and I went from Teased too Pleased. My declaration today is "I have the sanctified touch and I don't want to lose it." God was preparing me in grammar school for what would take place in high school.

When I got to high school, there were other saved children there who went to church and dressed like me. We rallied together to witness to our peers, and we won souls for Christ in school. God has a purpose and a plan for everything we go through.

"Let Your Hurt Push You to God"

In the Biblical narrative of Hannah, we see a person who was teased, how she handled it, and how the experience ultimately pushed her to God. The story of Hannah is found in 1 Samuel, chapters 1 and 2 (NIRV). Hannah is one of two wives of Elkanah. The other was Peninnah, who had given birth to Elkanah's children. Hannah remained childless because the Lord had shut up her womb. Nevertheless, Elkanah preferred Hannah, he loved her. Jealous of her favor,

Penninah teased Hannah to make her angry because she was barren. Annually, Elkanah took his family to the temple for worship. Childless, year after year Hannah endured Peninnah's teasing until her emotional pain became physical. She cried endlessly. Concerned, her husband would speak to her: "Hannah why are you crying? Why don't you eat? Why are you so unhappy? Don't I mean more to you more than ten sons?" Still, Hannah was inconsolable.

At some point, I believe that Hannah had enough. Her hurt and pain pushed her to the only one who could change her situation. She cried out to God. Hannah was in bitterness of soul, she prayed unto the lord and wept sore. She made a promise to God that if he would give her a son, she would give him back to God all the days of his life. God answered her prayer, and she gave birth to a son that they named "Samuel."

Sometimes God will allow us to go through difficult situations, and he uses our experiences ultimately to draw us to him. Just like Hannah, we must allow our hurt, our pain, and our disappointments to draw us to God. I like the fact that Hannah didn't allow Peninnah's teasing to keep her from showing up to worship. Some of us would have taken matters into our own hands, but Hannah never even tried to defend herself. Year after year, she kept showing up.

No matter what you are going through or dealing with right now, keep showing up for worship, keep going to church, keep praying, and allow God to heal you where you hurt.

A Battle with Fear

I had a battle with fear round 1 and lost. As a child I was very shy and was afraid to speak publicly. I was extremely uncomfortable every time I had to stand before people. When we were growing up, in church for Easter and Christmas, we had to recite speeches. I very quickly would learn my speeches, but when it came time for the programs and they would call my name, fear would overwhelm me, I often would cry through it because I was so afraid.

One day at school I had to recite a poem. I was so nervous but managed to get through it. The school librarian was in my classroom at the time. Not knowing that we were being judged, at the end of our class she excitedly announced that I had won the competition—she wanted me to represent the class and recite a poem in front of the entire school. Oh no, this was not good news for me. I instantly got nervous and scared. When I got home, I told my parents that I was chosen to represent my class and recite a poem at one of our assemblies in front of the entire school. I told them that I didn't want to do it because I was so afraid to speak in front of people.

My father, who was my biggest encourager, said to me, "Girl, what is that? That's nothing for you to do because you're my child." The fear that I had didn't immediately go away but his encouragement gave me the courage to try.

The day came when I was to recite the poem; I walked on stage to an audience that was full of teachers, staff, and students, and I pretty much choked. I stumbled over all my words, I was so embarrassed, and I never wanted to get up in front of people again. The things that you struggle with as a child, if left unchecked, will follow you into adulthood.

At the age of twenty-one I was called by God to be a missionary. This is something that I really did not want to do. I was already uncomfortable speaking in front of a crowd, but you mean to tell me now, I was being called to do something publicly that I absolutely didn't want to do? Even with these feelings, I never wanted to say "no" to God. The words to one of my favorite songs at the time was by the late Milton Brunson: "Never say no to Jesus, your answer should always be yes because when God gave his Son he didn't say no. For when he gave, he gave his best."

Despite all that, it seemed as though every time I had to bring a sermon, fear and anxiety would show. It was difficult to hear from God—to even know what to speak about—because ultimately, fear and anxiety disconnected me from hearing from him. It seemed that I was in spiritual warfare every single time I had to speak or do anything publicly for that matter. I battled with fear for a long time. I would often cancel and say I just can't do it. John 10:10a says, "The thief cometh not, but for to steal, and to kill, and to destroy" (KJV). The enemy tried to use fear to take me out of the presence of God as he was trying to steal my destiny.

What causes fear? Unbelief. Fear is the enemy of faith. Where there is fear and unbelief, you are not trusting God. I was reading my Bible, but I wasn't applying it because my fears were louder than my faith. The enemy will have you second-guessing things in life that God has ordained. The devil was literally trying to steal my faith. I was in a spiritual battle, but I had to fight to win through prayer, fasting, and believing. "I sought the Lord, and he heard me, and delivered me from all my fears" (Psalm 34:4, KJV).

Dressed Up and Messed Up

Every day we make a conscious decision to get up and get dressed. We decide each day what we are going to wear. I find that sometimes what we choose to put on camouflages how we really feel. I try to dress a little better on the days that I am not feeling my best to keep others from noticing, hoping that if I dress better than I feel, I will feel better than I'm dressed. So many times, we are dressed up on the outside but because of life's circumstances we are crying and broken on the inside. Some are dressed up and hurting, dressed up and burdened, dressed up and depressed, dressed up and fearful. Sometimes we are going to church, functioning in ministry, but are in a place of brokenness. We're helping others, praying for others, ministering to others and they are being healed and blessed, but it seems as though God has us on hold.

Have you ever been in a place where you were praying and calling on the name of Jesus, but you couldn't feel him, you couldn't trace him, and you couldn't hear him? I was never hurt as much in life as when I went through this season of drought. I was in a dry place in my life, still functioning in ministry dressed up on the outside, and messed up with fear on the inside. I was reaching out for God but it seemed that he was not there.

This season of my life went on for a while. It's one thing to be hurt by others but there is absolutely no hurt worse than when you feel abandoned by God. How did I get here? What transpired in my life that caused me to feel disconnected from God? It was fear, the same fear that started in my childhood. I asked the question many times, "Lord, where are you?"

I related my experience to Job 23:8-10 (KJV), "Behold, I go forward, but he is not there; and backward, but I cannot perceive him: On the left hand, where he doth work, but I cannot behold him: he hideth himself on the right hand, that I cannot see him: But he knoweth the way that I take: when he hath tried me, I shall come forth as gold."

This was another time in my life where God was driving me to him. He was inviting me to have a closer relationship with him. The more abandoned I felt, the more it drove me to seek him. In my desert, I began to fast and pray often, reminding God of his Word. I would say things like "Lord, you said that you would never leave me nor forsake me." "Lord, you said that nothing can separate me from your Love."

I began quoting many other scriptures that resonated in me. At some point, I realized that the scripture reminders weren't for God. God already knows what he said. The scripture reminders were for me; he just wanted me to believe.

When we are praying while going through our desert experiences, God just wants to know if we believe him. Even if he doesn't answer right away, he's asking, "Will you trust me, believe my word, and not give up?" Most believers answer, "Yes, Lord I trust you; I believe your Word." Yet sometimes, what we say so well, we live so poorly. Hebrews 11:6 says, "But without faith it is impossible to please him: for he that cometh to God must believe that he is, and that he is a rewarder of them that diligently seek him" (KJV).

God spoke to me in prayer and told me "Believe." This word alone helped me to not give up. I knew at that moment that God had heard my prayer and all I had to do is believe and wait on him.

It was faith, prayer, and my praise that lifted me up out of this valley. I went from dressed up and messed up, to dressed up and prayed up. We must allow God to do the dressing. Ephesians 6:11 says, "Put on the whole armor of God, that ye may be able to stand against the wiles of the devil" (KJV). Whatever you're dressed up with that doesn't fit the armor of God, get rid of it. We can't win a spiritual battle in the flesh.

In my quest of seeking the Lord, I was crying out to him, and it was during this time that a praise and worship song was birthed. I began to sing these words to God:

> In your presence is where I love to be.
> Walk beside me and I'll claim the victory.
> In your presence there's fullness of joy.
> In your presence is where I love to be.

The more I sang the words to this song, the more of God's presence I felt. In round 2 of my battle with fear, I not only won, but I defeated fear with my faith.

Have No Fear: Jesus Is Here

During this fight, many times I quoted 2 Timothy 1:7, "For God has not given us the spirit of fear; but of power, and of love, and of a sound mind" (KJV). Timothy in the Bible also struggled with the spirit of fear. It seemed that a lack of confidence or being too timid was sometimes a problem for him. Just like Timothy, we don't have to rely on our own strength to fulfill the ministry that God has given us. Whatever God calls us to do we have no reason to fear, because God never calls us to a task which he doesn't equip and enable us to fulfill. Trusting God is our weapon against the enemy's fear and doubt. Fear had a hold on me, but it had to release me because God had a greater plan for me. I conquered and prevailed over fear with faith.

Years later, in 2005, who knew that God would have me bring a sermon on fear. My topic was "Have No Fear: Jesus Is Here." I took my text from Matthew 14:27, "But straightway Jesus spake unto them, saying, Be of good cheer; it is I; be not afraid" (KJV). We know that when Jesus shows up, he shows up with what we need. Since then, I have brought this sermon several times as we always need that reminder.

Just like me, you may struggle with fear. Whether your fears are natural, spiritual, mental, or physical, the fight against fear is a spiritual battle. Our weapon is the word of God. No matter what your fears are you can overcome them. Once conquered, the residue of fear may try to stick up its ugly head (because the enemy always try to come back where he was last successful), but you can beat it back down with your faith. Isaiah 41:10 says, "Fear thou not; for I am with thee: be not dismayed; for I am your God: I will strengthen thee; yea, I will help thee; yea, I will uphold thee with the right hand of my righteousness" (KJV).

Hurt but Not Harmed

We all at one time or another may have gone through something hurtful, but it wasn't necessarily harmful. Let us walk through the story of Joseph and see how he experienced hurt. But more importantly, let us focus on how he handled it, because all that he went through didn't harm him because God was with him.

In the book of Genesis, chapters 37 and 39–50, you will find the story of Joseph.

Joseph was no stranger to feeling pain and rejection as he experienced it from his very own brothers. At an early age, he had to deal with the pain of betrayal. Joseph was the eleventh son born to Jacob in his old age. He was the first-born child of Rachel, the wife that Jacob loved. The young Joseph, who was seventeen at the time, was a tattletale. When he would feed the flock with his brothers he would come back and tell his father all the evil that his brothers had done. Jacob loved Joseph more than all his children and made him a coat of many colors. The favor of his father caused Jacob's brothers to hate him. Showing favoritism among children will always cause conflict. To top it all off, Joseph had two dreams that implied that one day his brothers—and even his parents—would bow before him. This caused his brothers to hate him even more. (You must be careful whom you tell your dreams to because everyone cannot handle what God is about to do in your life.)

One day, Joseph's brothers went to feed their father's flock and as usual their father sent Joseph to check on them. When the brothers saw Joseph coming, they plotted to kill him, and they would have, but the oldest brother Reuben talked them out of it. He suggested that they put Joseph in a pit instead, secretly planning to come back later, get Joseph and bring him back to his father. When Joseph got to his brothers, they stripped him out of his coat and cast him into a pit. Another brother, Judah, spoke up and suggested they sell Joseph to the Ishmaelites. Joseph was sold into slavery by his very own brothers. I can only imagine the hurt and pain that this caused him. Betrayal is never easy, but it hurts even more when it comes from those who are the closest to you.

The brothers took Joseph's coat, killed a goat, and dipped it in blood. They took it back to their father and asked if the coat belonged to Joseph. He recognized the coat as his son's and assumed that a wild beast had devoured him. Jacob mourned for Joseph many days, and all of his daughters and sons tried to comfort him but he refused to be comforted. Some people don't want to get over their hurt; they would rather hold on to it. Jacob said that he would go to the grave mourning for his son. The deception of Jacob's sons caused him to hurt and mourn over something that was not true. He was hurting over something that never happened. Sometimes you're hurting over nothing. It's the things that the enemy puts in your mind or even your own assumptions that you allow to hurt you. Don't allow your thoughts to lead you down a path that doesn't exist and cause you unnecessary pain. Have you ever been in a place where you thought somebody said or did something and later found out that it wasn't true? The thoughts that you allowed even caused you to tell others. How did it affect you? Did you go the person and ask for forgiveness? Or did you just go on with life like Joseph's brothers, allowing their father to believe a lie? Although it's hard sometimes to admit our wrongs, it is necessary to be healed.

Joseph was sold by the Ishmaelites to the Egyptians to Potiphar, an officer of Pharaoh and captain of the guard. The Bible lets us know that the Lord was with Joseph and caused him to prosper in everything that he did. Potiphar put Joseph over all his household, and as a result, his house was blessed. Joseph was a very handsome young man, and Potiphar's wife soon began to make advances toward him. This behavior went on day in and day out, but Joseph rejected her advances. Joseph even ran away from her, leaving his coat behind. When she saw that his coat was in her hand, she falsely accused Joseph of making advances toward her.

Have you ever been falsely accused? It is one of the worst hurts ever. It's never easy when others believe a lie over the truth. In a lot of cases, people don't investigate, or even come to you, to see if it's true. You are basically guilty until proven innocent.

This is what happened to Joseph. As a result of a lie, Potiphar put him in prison, but the Lord was with Joseph and gave him favor with the keeper of the prison. The keeper of the prison put Joseph over all the prisoners. It is always easier to go through your trials and your tribulations knowing that the Lord is with you.

While in prison, Joseph met Pharaoh's butler and baker, and each man had a dream. Joseph was able to interpret the dream, and they came true just as he said. Two years later, Pharaoh had a dream that no one else could interpret but Joseph. The meaning of Pharaoh's dream was that there would be seven years of plenty and seven years of famine. The interpretation of the dream pleased Pharaoh so much that he promoted Joseph to second in command over Egypt and put him in charge of the entire land. God gave Joseph wisdom on what to do during the time of plenty so they could survive the famine. Pharaoh's dream came to pass exactly the way that Joseph interpreted it.

As the famine grew worse, Jacob, Joseph's father, sent his sons to Egypt to buy food. When Joseph's brothers arrived in Egypt and bowed before him, he quickly recognized them; however, they didn't recognize him. It was at this time that Joseph could have taken revenge on them. He could have gotten them back for mistreating him and for selling him into slavery. But instead, Joseph chose forgiveness. He even told them not to be angry with themselves that they sold him, because God had sent him there before them to preserve life.

Look at all that Joseph went through: he was thrown into a pit, he was sold into slavery, he was falsely accused, he was forgotten, and then he was remembered and ultimately, he made it to the palace—his place of promotion—and his dreams were fulfilled.

What we go through may be in God's plan, but how we handle it determines our outcome. I never read where Joseph had a pity party or that he felt sorry for himself, but I believe that Joseph knew that God was with him every step of the way. Please know that when you are going through your trials and tribulations, the Lord is with you. Joseph had to go through the process, he didn't get there overnight. Joseph was 17 when he had his dreams; however, he was 30 when he became governor of Egypt. Just like Joseph, we must go through the process to get to the place where God is trying to take us. There's purpose to your pain if you keep the faith and don't give up. I call it the pain of becoming.

When Joseph's father died, the brothers thought that Joseph would hate them and get them back for all the evil that they had done to him. So, they sent a messenger to Joseph saying that their father told them to ask him for forgiveness for all of the evil that they had done against him. This caused Joseph to weep. His brothers bowed before him saying that they were willing to be his servants. Joseph's response was, "You intended to harm me, but God intended it for good to accomplish what is now being done, the saving of many lives" (Genesis 50:20 NIV). Joseph was hurt but not harmed because what he went through was all in God's plan. Your hurt is going to help if you keep the faith.

Romans 12:19 says, "Dearly beloved, avenge not yourselves, but rather give place unto wrath: for it is written, Vengeance is mine; I will repay, saith the Lord" (KJV).

You never have to take revenge on anyone. "Since God is going to take up your cause and see to it that justice is done, you can let it go. You don't have to carry anger, bitterness, or resentment."

(John Piper—"God's Wrath 'Vengeance Is Mine, I Will Repay,'" February 27, 2005, https://www.desiringgod.org/messages/gods-wrath)

Reflection

Forgiveness Is Essential to Be Healed

What is forgiveness? Why is it necessary to forgive the person who hurt you? They mistreated you, so why do you have to forgive them when you are hurting? At some point in our lives, we've had to forgive or had to ask for forgiveness. At times we were the offender and at other times we were offended. Why then is it so hard for some to forgive when they themselves want to be forgiven? Anyone who has a hard time forgiving needs to be reminded of what God has forgiven them from. The same grace that you want from God, is the same grace that you must be willing to give.

Mark 11:25 (KJV) says, "And when ye stand praying, forgive, if ye have ought against any: that your Father also which is in heaven may forgive you your trespasses."

You must forgive, to be forgiven. I find that sometimes people don't want to forgive because they feel that the person is getting away with what they did. We must understand that when we forgive it does not excuse the fact that what happened took place, rather it uncages the prison of your mind, so you do not repeat that incident over and over again. You must face it, you may have to face them, and you must let it go.

I interviewed someone who shared that as a believer she struggled with unforgiveness for about 20 years. The person experienced a lot of hurt and pain because as a child she always wanted to have a relationship with her father. However, her father never showed up for her in her life. The hurtful part was that the father had other children that he was there for and this daughter couldn't understand why he was never there for her, especially when he lived right down the street from her. She would see him pretty much every day; he would be with his other children but would always avoid her.

Although her uncle, her father's brother, would always come around, buy things, and spend time with her, his presence still didn't take the place of her wanting so badly to have a relationship with her father. She couldn't get over the hurt and pain of him not being in her life. This is quite devastating for a child.

Her mother got married when she was 13 years old. Her stepfather bought her first bike. He taught her how to drive and a lot of other things. He also spent quality time with her, which helped fill some of the void left by her father.

The hurt and pain that she experienced from her father's rejection caused her to build walls. She felt that she had to protect herself now from any and every person who could possibly hurt her. The unforgiveness that was in her heart for her dad spilled over into other relationships. She felt that people would deliberately do and say things to hurt her or to try to bring her down. She would hold a grudge against anyone who wronged her instead of releasing it.

After 20 years of holding grudges pretty much against everyone that hurt her, God began to deal with her heart. She understood that she had to forgive. She realized that this was nothing that she could do on her own. Every day she would pray, "Lord forgive me and help me to forgive." She said that the grudge didn't go away immediately, but she kept praying and one day she realized that she was free. She could see her dad and others who hurt her, but it no longer affected her because God healed her where she was hurting. He released her from the hurt that held her hostage and now she is walking in freedom. When we walk in freedom, the chains of hurt no longer imprison us, and we can freely love those who caused us pain.

Forgiveness is not for the person who offended or hurt you; forgiveness is for you. It frees you from the offense, and that person or situation no longer has power over you. Unforgiveness is classified in medical books as a disease. Dr. Karen Swartz, M.D., is the director of Clinical and Educational Programs at the Johns

Hopkins Mood Disorders Center. In "Forgiveness: Your Health Depends on It," Dr. Swartz said, "There is an enormous physical burden to being hurt and disappointed." The article from Johns Hopkins Medicine further states:

> Chronic anger puts you into a fight-or-flight mode, which results in numerous changes in heart rate, blood pressure and immune response. Those changes, then, increase the risk of depression, heart disease and diabetes, among other conditions. Forgiveness, however, calms stress levels, leading to improved health. (Johns Hopkins Medicine, https://www.hopkinsmedicine.org/health/wellness-and-prevention/forgiveness-your-health-depends-on-it,

I am not saying that forgiveness is always easy, and for some it's a process. However, it's something that you must do in order to be healed.

Reflection

The Bruises of Life

The other day I noticed a bruise on my arm, and I didn't quite know how it got there, but I knew that it didn't just appear. Something had to take place for it to be there. It was amazing to me that a bruise that I didn't know existed did not hurt until I discovered it and touched it. In the same way that we discover pain from physical bruises, we can also discover pain from what I call "the bruises of life." Those bruises sometimes just show up when we least expect it.

You may have seen someone or something or had a thought that reminded you of a painful experience you thought you were over. The reminder stirred something up in your heart, letting you know that the bruise is still there. In that moment, it perhaps brought anger, hurt, frustration, and pain. It caused you to react and it was evident that your bruises were showing.

A bruise is something that just doesn't show up and disappear on the same day. A bruise has a way of lasting a while; it leaves a mark, and the force of the impact determines the size of the bruise. There are many bruises in life—the bruises of sickness, loss, hurts, trials, and tribulations. On this journey called life, you are going to experience some bruises, those tender moments that come along with great pain. However, the bruises that I would like to focus on in this chapter are the bruises of death.

Death is certain, but never easy. Death robs you from your loved ones but can't rob you from the memories. Hold on to the memories, the good times, the laughs, the joy that they brought you. "How do I cope?" you might ask. Take one day at a time. Although the effects of death have a way of lingering, however, each day it gets a little easier—especially when you walk it out with God. Even in death, God is with you and he can fill the void.

Sudden deaths seemingly are the toughest to handle. An unexpected loss that catches you off guard can sometimes be unbearable; it can lead you to crying out to God, asking, "Why?" Why my loved one? Why my friend? Why my co-worker? All of our why questions are answered the same way. It's God's will. Jesus himself struggled with God's will when he was in the Garden of Gethsemane. He prayed three times, "Father, if it be possible, let this cup pass from me. Nevertheless, not my will, but thy will be done" (Matthew 26:39 KJV paraphrased). Hold on to nevertheless and try to accept what God allows.

We have all at one time or another experienced hurt through the death of a loved one, a friend, or someone very dear to us. We know that healing from a loss of a loved one is a process. The initial pain that you feel is excruciating. Grief can shake you to your very core. It seems that when you first lose a loved one everyone is usually there: they're checking on you, praying for you, and visiting you, but when the funeral is over, everything tends to go back to normal. The phone calls, visits, and seemingly even the prayers stop. You're left to feel the reality of the pain of the loss of your loved one. Still, there is good news: even in this, God is still with you and he can ease the pain.

"Weeping may endure for a night but joy cometh in the morning" (Psalm 30:5, KJV). Sometimes we must cry it out to get it out.

Everyone's experience is different, as we all deal with death differently. many people can't cope with death. They become depressed; some lose their appetite. Some days they may even wake up crying. It appears the holidays are worse because you have to try to get over the initial reality that your loved one is no longer here, and never coming back. The effects of death have a way of lingering as the memory of your loved one comes and go. Some never get over it, and some even become angry with God. This doesn't have to be you.

The first loss of a close family member that I can remember was my sister who passed at the tender age of sixteen years old. Although I was only three years old, I still have very fond memories of her. I was even told that I was the one who found her when she passed away. I was very afraid of turning sixteen because for some reason I felt that I would pass away at that age also. Thank God he had other plans for me.

Years later, at 17 years old, I lost my father. My father was my hero; he was the pastor of our church, and he was also a family man. He always found time to spend with us. On Saturdays, we had movie night. My father would go to the library and borrow movies that we would watch on his projector. Dad was an encourager; he would always encourage us to do our best. My father always made his children feel that we could do anything, and it gave us the courage to try, as we wanted to make him proud.

My father took sick suddenly, and there was quite a bit going on in his body. I was holding on to hope that he would be healed, but God knows best. I will never forget June 16, 1987, on my father's birthday we got the call from the hospital that he had passed away. This was a day that changed my life. My dad, my encourager, my hero was gone. Life for me and my family would be so different now. I didn't really grieve my dad's death right away, although I was incredibly sad. I no longer wanted to attend funerals. Each one felt like I was reliving my father's homegoing service all over again.

It wasn't until Father's Day the very next year that his death hit me hard. We were in church and the choir sang a song by Edwin Hawkins. I still remember the words to the song "My Trust Lies in You":

> "Need a little sunshine
> For the rain has covered my soul
> Need a little bit of mending
> My heart, my heart has been broken but
> My trust, it lies in you."

I couldn't take it anymore. I went to the basement of the church and I could not stop weeping. To my surprise, my mom was there too, weeping. That was the first time that I saw my mom cry, which made me weep even more.

Although I felt so much better being able to get it out, I still didn't want to go to any more funerals. My mom allowed me to do this for a good while before she told me that I had to start going back to funerals because it was a part of life. I begrudgingly obeyed, but I was so afraid. I would come home and sleep with the lights on. Everything about death at the time was so scary to me. It was so final. You would never see that person again on this side of life. Who knew that years later, I would have the strength to witness someone taking their last breath, plan a funeral for a friend, serve as Mistress of Ceremonies for a funeral service, etc. I would have never thought that I would have ever had the courage to do so.

There were many sad moments that I had, and still have at times, missing my dad. One day that was particularly difficult was the day I got married. It hit me pretty hard that my dad wasn't going to be present to march me down the aisle. Most of us look forward to that special day. Just thinking about him on that day made me instantly sad, and it was in that moment that the bruises of my pain began to show. I began to long for my father; with tears in my eyes, I began to talk to the Lord and tell him in that moment that I needed him to be my father, because I no longer had one, and I needed him to fill the void.

I didn't want to get stuck in my grief as Jacob did when his sons deceived him and he refused to be comforted. I knew that I had to do something to pull myself out. This was a happy day for me. I began to think about the happy times that I shared with my father, and I knew that he would have been proud, and happy for me at the same time, and he would have wanted me to move forward and enjoy my new life with my husband. Therefore, I didn't stay in that moment. I did a special tribute in honor of my father and enjoyed my beautiful wedding. Thinking about the good memories still helps me to this day get through the bruises of death. Philippians 4:13 reminds us that "I can do all things through Christ which strengtheneth me" (KJV). In every sad moment that comes along with death, just know that God is your strength.

Reflection

Just Because It Hurts Doesn't Mean It Has to Dwell:

"Give Your Hurt to Jesus"

It is now time to release the hurt. You don't have to remain in a place where God never intended for you to be. If you dwell on something long enough, especially something painful, it affects you. You could be having a great day and suddenly a negative or painful thought comes to your mind, and you begin to think about it repeatedly. It can change your mood, your countenance, and even your behavior. You are now under its control. Others begin to feel the brunt of your hurt because you are now taking your anger and frustrations out on them. Don't allow bitterness to take residence in your heart and, by all means, don't become who hurt you. As the saying goes "Hurt people hurt people."

When a person has a serious injury, they go to the doctor. Someone who is a professional in that field must assist them in the healing process, and just like the natural doctor, there is a Balm in Gilead. We have a spiritual doctor who can heal you where you hurt. His name is Jesus, and he is the Chief Physician; he is the specialist of every hurt or wound that you can ever have. "He healeth the broken in heart, and bindeth up their wounds" (Psalm 147:3, KJV). "If you can have it, he can heal it." Jehovah Rapha he is our healer.

Step one: Release the hurt; let it go.

The first step in releasing the hurt is wanting to let go. God will honor what you surrender. You must make up in your mind that you don't ever want to be stuck in a place, where anything or anyone—including yourself—has boxed you in, all because you are not willing to let go. Don't get stuck in a place that hinders all the purpose that God has for your life. Some people are like caged-up birds that have been in a cage for so long that when someone opens the door, they remain inside. Why? Simply because the bird is used to being caged up, not knowing that all it must do is go through the open door and it will be free. Well, Jesus is the open door to your freedom. He can free you from that very thing that has held you hostage. However, God can't take what you're not willing to give. What does it mean to walk in freedom? Walking in freedom literally means letting go of any and everything that is holding you hostage.

Many times, the healing process has already begun but—just like that child who has a physical sore who keeps picking at it, causing it to bleed—we as adults, can keep picking at our emotional scars, and wounds, causing them to bleed all over again. You continue to relive the hurt. An open wound can only heal when you stop picking at it. Please understand that holding on to hurt only hurts you. You will know when you have released the hurt because the residue of the pain will no longer exist. If you keep talking about it and bringing it up, that means that it's still there. One of the worst parts of not letting go of your pain is every day you must live with it.

At some point, you must realize that you must do some soul searching and truly be honest with God letting him know that the hurt is there, and you want to release it. I do know that sometimes it is easier said than done. It may require you going to counseling, fasting, and praying and crying out to God for healing and deliverance. Sometimes this can be a process; it takes time. The first time you pray the pain may not go away; it depends on what it is, how long it's been there, and how deeply it has affected you. It also depends on your willingness to let go. Many times, when we pray and we are giving our issue to Jesus, we have the tendency of taking it back. We give it to the Lord, and we take it back. In order to be healed we must totally give our hurts, our burdens, our disappointments, our issues over to the Lord and leave them there. Casting all your care upon him; for he careth for you 1 Peter 5:7 (KJV). If it were something that you could have done in your own strength, it would be done by now.

At some point in this process, you have to say, "Enough is enough." You must tell yourself, "I am tired of crying over this, I am tired of carrying this burden, and I am tired of being complacent." Sometimes you can be your biggest hindrance. Your tiredness should lead you to act. When you are holding on to issues that you need to let go of—especially when working in ministry—you are not in a place spiritually where you can freely minister to others because you are bound yourself. God is a burden bearer and a heavy load sharer.

Step two: We must put our total trust in God.

Second, trust God. Proverbs 3:5 says, "Trust in the Lord with all thine heart; and lean not unto thine own understanding" (KJV).

"Trusting in the Lord with all your heart is the opposite of doubting and ignoring God and his word. It also involves surrendering our anxieties, our worries, hurts and fears to him. As God's children, we can be assured that our Heavenly Father loves us and he will faithfully care for us" (Fire Bible (KJV) Verse Commentary Proverbs 3:5).

We must lean on God and not ourselves. Hebrews 11:6 says, "But without faith it is impossible to please him: for he that cometh to

God must believe that he is, and that he is a rewarder of them that diligently seek him" (KJV).

"We must believe in the existence of a personal, infinite, holy God who cares for us. We must believe that God will respond to us when we sincerely look to him in faith, knowing that our greatest reward is the joy and presence of God himself" (Fire Bible (KJV) Verse Commentary Hebrews 11:6). We must trust God through it, knowing that he's able to bring us out.

This is how you begin to build your trust in God. Every day get a scripture on your heart and meditate on that scripture throughout the day. When bad experiences try to resurface, at that time begin to talk to God. Cry out to him. Meet him in prayer. Tell him, "Lord help me to trust you and your plan." I find, at times, to get over that moment you may have to stay on your knees in prayer until it lifts. If it doesn't lift right away, be honest with God and let him know that it's still there. There were times when I was faced with hurt, so I had to stay in prayer sometimes for a long time and I would say these words to God, "Take it Lord," and sometimes I would even sing it and our faithful God would take that hurt and that burden away. God may not always take it away, right away, because there are some things in it designed to mature us, and to grow us up in him.

Step three: Lord, do what's necessary in me.

Third, you must ask God to do what's necessary in you. God knows us much better than we know ourselves. He also knows if we are still holding on to things that we ourselves are not aware of. We must understand that God can make us over again. He is the potter, and we are the clay. He is well able to make us and mold us into what he wants us to be. Don't allow anything to remain in your heart that could potentially keep you from your breakthrough or healing. Jesus wants to heal you. Sometimes you may feel that you're already healed. It's OK to ask God to search your heart. Psalm 139:23-24 says, "Search me, O God, and know my heart: try me, and know my thoughts: And see if there be any wicked way in me, and lead me in the way everlasting" (KJV).

Give God full access to every part of you. We must be aware if there's something in us that grieves God. We should always be willing to let God put us through any test that would reveal hidden sins and hurts, and if you're holding on to any offense, ask God to take it away, cry out to God, and ask him to heal the place where only he knows is bleeding. You can be hemorrhaging on the inside with pain and not know it. God is omniscient; he's all knowing. He can wash you clean. He knows all about you. All you must do is give it to him and allow him to transform you.

Don't stay stuck in your hurt when you can be free. John 8:36 says, "If the son therefore shall make you free, ye shall be free indeed." Get in your word, develop a strong prayer life, humble yourself—you may even have to fast and pray until every chain of the enemy is broken. Give God your wounded heart; bring your hurts to Jesus. When you give your burdens, your issues, your problems, and your heartaches over to the Lord, that burden lifts, and you begin to walk in freedom and can receive all that God has for you. Cry out to him right now and allow God to heal you where you hurt. God is well able to take you "From Hurt to Healed."

Reflection

Conclusion

I remember working with a group of people who were giving me a hard time; they had conspired against me and were determined to fight everything that I was trying to implement. It seemed that I was wasting my time being there. I was sitting at my computer one day and was thinking about what I was going through. I said to myself, "I don't have to take this. I am just going to quit," but suddenly God got my attention through my computer. It started automatically updating and I hadn't even touched it. Can I tell it the way that it really happened? I asked my computer out loud, "Who told you to update?" So, I hit ESC, and at that moment a message flashed on my screen that I never saw before and have never seen since. The message said, "If you escape you will abort." Those words hit me so hard that I had to ask the question, "God is this you?" Sometimes we are trying to run away from the very thing that God has ordained. The computer updating was letting me know that God was updating/changing some things in me. Sometimes God must work some things in us and sometimes he must work some things out of us.

Nothing that we go through is ever wasted. Romans 8:28 says," And we know that all things work together for good to them that love God, to them who are the called according to his purpose" (KJV). I, like a lot of people, have prayed the prayer, "Lord, make me and mold me in the way that you want me to be." However, I quickly learned that we can't tell him how to do it. People may give you a hard time—they may even mistreat you—but I believe that we are tested on how well we handle it.

I left my desk, got on my knees and began to pray and praise God for the test. In a matter of minutes, I went from hurt to praise. After prayer, three scriptures came to mind: the first part of Psalm 46:10, "Be still and know that I am God;" 2 Timothy 2:3, "Thou therefore endure hardness, as a good soldier of Jesus Christ;" and Psalm 27:14, "Wait on the Lord: be of good courage, and he shall strengthen thine heart: wait, I say, on the Lord" (KJV). I believe that the Lord was saying to me: Be still, endure, and wait.

Although things didn't change right away, God gave me the strength to make it through. God doesn't always take us out of the trial, but he has a way of changing us in it. This trial taught me that sometimes you need to be delivered from people.

"Lord deliver me from people so I can see you.

They're blocking my view"

to be continued....

Reflection

Healing Scriptures to Meditate On

He healeth the broken in heart, and bindeth up their wounds Psalm 147:3, KJV.

Confess your faults one to another, and pray one for another, that ye may be healed. The effectual fervent prayer of a righteous man availeth much James 5:16, KJV.

But he was wounded for our transgressions, he was bruised for our iniquities: the chastisement of our peace was upon him; and with his stripes we are healed Isaiah 53:5, KJV.

Fear thou not; for I am with thee: be not dismayed; for I am thy God: I will strengthen thee; yea, I will help thee; yea, I will uphold thee with the right hand of my righteousness Isaiah 41:10, KJV.

The Lord is nigh unto them that are of a broken heart; and saveth such as be of a contrite spirit Psalm 34:18, KJV.

The Lord shall fight for you, and ye shall hold your peace Exodus 14:14, KJV.

Dearly beloved, avenge not yourselves, but rather give place unto wrath: for it is written, Vengeance is mine; I will repay, saith the Lord Romans 12:19, KJV.

And be ye kind one to another, tenderhearted, forgiving one another, even as God for Christ's sake hath forgiven you Ephesians 4:32, KJV.

For I know the thoughts that I think toward you, saith the Lord, thoughts of peace, and not of evil, to give you an expected end Jeremiah 29:11, KJV.

A Call to Salvation

If you don't know Jesus in the pardon of your sins, this is a good time to give your life to the Lord. Please repeat these words from a sincere heart:

> Father forgive me, for every sin that I ever committed.
>
> Wash my heart, wash my mind, and wash my soul.
>
> Thank you for dying for my sins.
>
> Satan, I denounce you and accept you Jesus as my Lord and savior.
>
> Thank you, Jesus, for saving me.

"That if thou shalt confess with thy mouth the Lord Jesus, and shalt believe in thine heart that God hath raised him from the dead, thou shalt be saved" Romans 10:9 (KJV).

www.ingramcontent.com/pod-product-compliance
Lightning Source LLC
Chambersburg PA
CBHW071223160426
43196CB00012B/2394